Key Stage 2
Mathematics
Assessment
Papers

for the
National Curriculum

ANSWERS

Schofield & Sims

1

4 rules to 2 decimal places/check with inverse or approximation

Work out each of the following and show how you would check your answer.

45.36 + 28.7	79.08 − 35.9	209.7 × 8	630.84 ÷ 7
74.06	**43.18**	**1677.6**	**90.12**
Check	Check	Check	Check

Checks may	*be made by*	*approximation*	*or inverse*
<u>approx</u>	<u>approx</u>	<u>approx</u>	<u>approx</u>
45 + 30 = 75	79 − 36 = 43	200 × 8 =1600	630 ÷ 7 = 90
<u>inverse</u>	<u>inverse</u>	<u>inverse</u>	<u>inverse</u>
74.06	43.18		90.12
− 28.70	+ 35.9	209.7	× 7
45.36	79.08	8)1677.6	630.84

2

Long multiplication and division (3-digit by 2-digit number)

```
   345
 ×  60
 _____
 20700
```

```
        1 9
  40 )7 6 0
```

```
        8
  74 )5 9 2
```

```
   478
 ×  97
 _____
 46366
```

```
       2 0.9
  30 )6 2 7
```

```
       2 9
  27 )7 8 3
```

A.T.2 – Number Developing methods of computation

3 **Calculate fractional parts of quantities/measures**

Calculate each of the following.

half of 97	$\frac{3}{4}$ of 76	one third of 84 g	five sixths of 1.74 m
48.5	$(\frac{1}{4} = 19)$ $\frac{3}{4} = 57$	28 g	$(\frac{1}{6} = 0.29\ m)$ $\frac{5}{6} = 1.45\ m$

one twelfth of 3 hours	one tenth of 25 litres	five sevenths of 1 week	three tenths of 2 kg
15 min	2.5 litres	5 days	600 g

4 **Calculate percentage parts of quantities/measures**

Calculate each of the following.

25% of 300	10% of 35	50% of 18	75% of 12
75	3.5	9	9

20% of 95	$33\frac{1}{3}$ % of 99	$12\frac{1}{2}$ % of 48	5% of 80
19	33	6	4

5 | Multiply whole numbers and decimals by 10, 100, 1000

Multiply these numbers by 10.

2.1 → | 21 | 2.01 → | 20.1 | 200.1 → | 2001 | 0.02 → | 0.2 |

Multiply these numbers by 100.

17.0 → | 1700 | 0.17 → | 17 | 1.07 → | 107 | 10.07 → | 1007 |

Multiply these numbers by 1000.

3.04 → | 3040 | 3.40 → | 3400 | 0.34 → | 340 | 340.0 → | 340 000 |

6 | Divide whole numbers and decimals by 10, 100, 1000

Divide these numbers by 10.

89 → | 8.9 | 809 → | 80.9 | 8.09 → | 0.809 | 8.90 → | 0.89 |

Divide these numbers by 100.

47 → | 0.47 | 4.7 → | 0.047 | 4.07 → | 0.0407 | 40.70 → | 0.407 |

Divide these numbers by 1000.

305 → | 0.305 | 3.05 → | 0.00305 |

0.35 → | 0.00035 | 350.0 → | 0.35 |

A.T.1 – Using and Applying Mathematics   Developing Mathematical language and forms of communication

A.T.2 – Number   Developing an understanding of place value and extending the number system

7

Compare two distributions, range, mean

Graph to show maximum and minimum temperatures for one week.

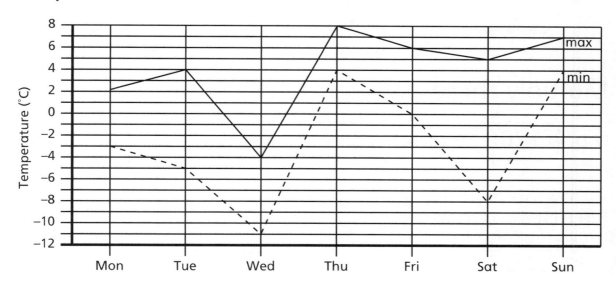

Which day had the biggest temperature range?

Saturday

What was the mean maximum temperature for the week?

4°C

Which day did the temperature not rise above zero?

Wednesday

Add/subtract negative numbers in context

Complete the following table using the above graph.

Day	Max. Temp (°C)	Min. Temp (°C)	Range	Mean Temp. (°C)
Mon	2	−3	5°C	−0.5°C
Tue	4	−5	9°C	−0.5°C
Wed	−4	−11	7°C	−7.5°C
Thur	8	4	4°C	6°C
Fri	6	0	6°C	3°C
Sat	5	−8	13°C	−1.5°C
Sun	7	4	3°C	5.5°C

A.T.4 – Handling Data

Collecting, representing and interpreting data
Understanding and using probability

8

Construct a formula from a pattern, express a formula in symbols

This square has sides of 1 cm.

Its perimeter is [4] cm.

This shape is made from 2 of the squares.

Its perimeter is [6] cm.

The perimeter of this shape is [8] cm.

Draw the next shape in the series.

Its perimeter is [10] cm.

Complete the following table.

Number of squares	1	2	3	4	5	6	7	8	9
Perimeter	4	6	8	10	12	14	16	18	20

What is the perimeter of the shape made with 50 squares?

50 + 50 + 2 =   102 cm

How did you work out the answer?

Double the number of squares and add 2

If the number of 1 cm squares is **n** and the perimeter of the shape is **P**, write a formula for finding the perimeter of any number of squares in the pattern.

$$P = 2n + 2$$

A.T.1 – Using and Applying Mathematics
A.T.2 – Number

Developing Mathematical reasoning
Understanding relationships between numbers

9 | **Use simple formulae (1 or 2 steps)**

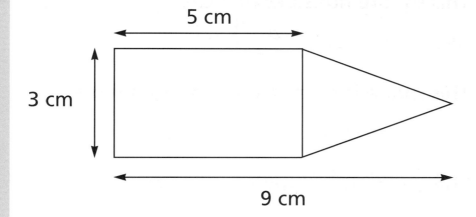

Area of a triangle = $\frac{1}{2}$ (base × height)

Find the area of the triangle shown above.

> height of triangle is 9 – 5 = 4 cm
>
> $\frac{1}{2}$ × 3 × 4 = 6 cm^2

What is the area of the whole shape?

> area of rectangle   is   15 cm^2
> + area of triangle   6 cm^2
> _____
>   21 cm^2

10 Convert one metric unit to another

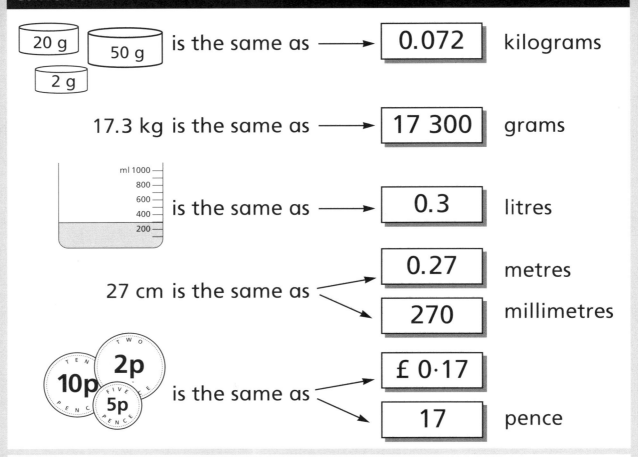

20 g 50 g 2 g **is the same as** ⟶ 0.072 kilograms

17.3 kg is the same as ⟶ 17 300 grams

ml 1000 800 600 400 200 **is the same as** ⟶ 0.3 litres

27 cm is the same as 0.27 metres / 270 millimetres

10p 2p 5p **is the same as** £ 0·17 / 17 pence

11

A gardener wishes to make a trellis for his roses.

He needs to buy wooden strips 25 mm wide.

He would like the spaces between the wooden strips to be exactly 20 cm squares.

He would like the finished height to be as near to 2 m as possible.

How high should he make the trellis?
Show your working here.

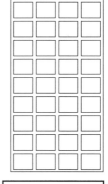

2.05 m

(There are many possible ways to work out the answer. Make sure the child can cope with the equivalence of the different measurements.)
2 metres would allow 10 spaces exactly with no strips.
Therefore, the trellis must have fewer spaces.
1 space + 1 strip measures 22.5 cm.
Try 9 (9 × 22.5) + 2.5 = 205 cm
Try 8 (8 × 22.5) + 2.5 = 182.5 cm, i.e. 9 is nearer 2 m.

A.T.3 – Shape, Space and Measures Understanding and using measures

12 | **Rough Imperial**

Complete the following table and tick whether your estimate is slightly larger or slightly smaller than the Imperial measure.

Imperial measure	rough metric equivalent	The metric measure is slightly larger	slightly smaller
yard	(1 metre) 90 cm	(✓)	✓
foot	30 cm		✓
inch	25 mm/2.5 cm		✓
gallon	4.5 litres		✓
pint	500 ml		✓
pound	500 g	✓	
mile	1500 m		✓

An old recipe for a delicious cake gives you all the quantities in Imperial measures. If you wished to make the cake today, what would the rough metric quantities be? Fill in this table.

Imperial	Metric
1 lb flour	500 g
8 oz margarine	250 g
4 oz sugar	125 g
12 oz dried fruit	375 g
$\frac{1}{2}$ pint water	250 ml
bake in an 8 inch tin	20 cm tin

13

Numerical problems as computation

chocolate biscuits	margarine	apples	milk
6 for £1·08	1 kg for £1·20	loose 56p/lb	1 litre for 58p
8 + 1 free £1·71	500 g for 62p	packs £1·12/kg	1 pint for 29p

Which way of buying each item is the better buy?

Item	better buy	reason
biscuits	6 for £1·08	£1·08 ÷ 6 = 18p each £1·71 ÷ 9 = 19p each
margarine	1 kg for £1·20	2 × 500 g = 1 kg So 1 kg at £1·20 2 × 62p = £1·24 is 4p cheaper
apples	1 kg for £1·12	2 lb apples is slightly less in mass than 1 kg but the cost is the same
milk	1 pint for 29p	2 pints is slightly more than 1 litre but costs the same

At the checkout, the bar-code reader is not working properly so the operator enters the items manually.
Your bill comes to £32·40. You only have £10 with you.
What do you do? Explain below.

You check your bill and find that you have been charged £29 instead of 29p for the milk. You explain this politely to the operator!

Your till receipt

```
biscuits          1·08
1 kg apples       1·12
1 pint milk      29·00
1 kg margarine    1·20
total amount     32·40
```

A.T.1 – Using and Applying Mathematics Making and monitoring decisions to solve problems

A checkout operator can serve 30 customers an hour.

What is the average time spent per customer?

> 60 ÷ 30
> = 2 minutes

The average bill per customer is £36·79.
What are the average hourly takings per operator?

> £36·79 × 30
> = £1103·70

At busy times 20 operators are employed.
What are the expected hourly takings at busy times?

> £1103·70 × 20
> = £22 074

One bar-code reader is faulty and the checkout operator can serve only 19 people per hour. On average, how much is lost by the store per hour?

> £36·79 × 19 = £699·01
> £1103·70 − £699·01
> = £404·69 lost (on average)
>
> (Can also use £36·79 x 11 as 11 customers are lost.)

A.T.1 – Using and Applying Mathematics Making and monitoring decisions to solve problems
A.T.2 – Number   Solving numerical problems

11

14

Construct models and draw shapes using angles to the nearest degree

Make a careful drawing of the triangle shown.

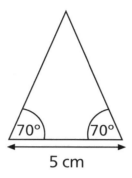

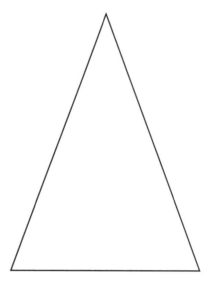

How many such triangles would you need
to make a model of a square-based pyramid?

4

Sketch the net you would use to make the pyramid.
(Ignore any fixing tabs.)

There are several possibilities for the answer.
Here are two:

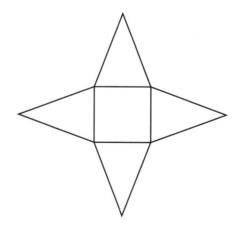

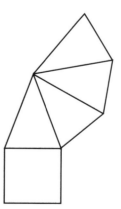

A.T.3 – Shape and Space
Understanding and using properties of shape
Understanding and using properties of position and movement

15 | **Identify all the symmetries of 2D shapes/Use angle language**

Draw all the lines of symmetry on these shapes.

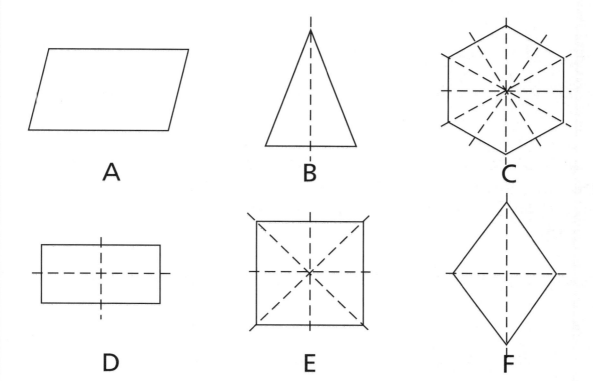

A   B   C

D   E   F

Now identify the order of rotational symmetry of each shape and complete the table below.

Shape	Name of shape	Order of rotational symmetry
A	parallelogram	2
B	(isosceles) triangle	1
C	(regular) hexagon	6
D	rectangle	2
E	square	4
F	diamond (or rhombus)	2

Which shapes contain obtuse angles?   A, C, F

Which shape contains only acute angles?   B

16 Probability scale 0 to 1/Justify outcomes

Class 4 visit the fairground.

Win a teddy
20p a go!

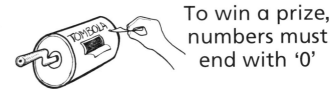

To win a prize,
numbers must
end with '0'

A tombola drum contains all the numbers from 1 to 1000. You can win a teddy if the number you pick ends with zero. If you have a go, what is the probability of winning a teddy?

Show your answer by marking a cross on the scale below.

```
0                          0.5                      1
|   X   |   |   |   |   |   |   |   |   |   |
```

A stall at the fairground is selling teddy bears.

 Teddy bears
£1·99 each

Amy would really like a teddy more than anything else, but she only has £2·00 to spend.

Should she buy a teddy or hope to win one on the tombola?

To be sure of having a teddy she should buy one.

Give your reasons.

She could have up to 10 goes on the tombola and still not win, or she could win and still have money left. The only certain way to get a teddy is to buy one.

Interpret pie charts, draw conclusions

There are 40 children in Class 4.
This pie chart shows their favourite rides.

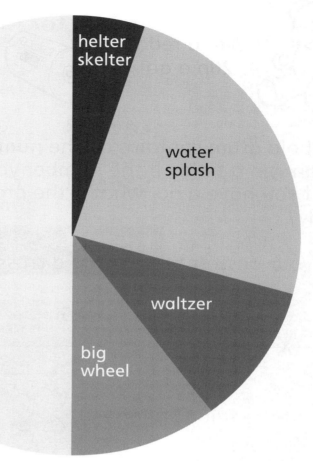

Which ride is the least popular?

| helter skelter |

What percentage of children
like the big dipper?

| 50% |

Which ride is liked by $\frac{1}{4}$ of
the children?

| water splash |

Which rides are liked by the
same number of children?

| waltzer, big wheel |

10% of the children like
the waltzer.
How many children is this?

| 4 |

A.T.4 – Handling Data   Collecting, representing and interpreting data
                                 Understanding and using probability

These papers are based on the Programmes of Study in **Mathematics** at **Key Stage 2**. They provide a wide variety of assessment opportunities in Mathematics skills, knowledge and understanding.

They are designed as an aid to the teacher's judgement when assessing a child's progress and deciding on levels of achievement. Therefore they should be used within the context of the teacher's knowledge of individual children.

They are not prescriptive in determining levels, but offer valuable indicators to depth and width of ability. Nor are they intended to be sole markers of attainment at any level and it is not anticipated that every child will succeed in every exercise offered in the different skills before being awarded a particular level.

They are a useful aid in planning and in work preparation and differentiation. They also provide a valuable record of progress when informing colleagues or reporting to parents.

Teachers should give help and explanation to children who do not understand initial instructions. Spare paper should be provided for any working out.

© 1997 Schofield & Sims Ltd.

First printed 1997.
Reprinted 1997 (twice).
Reprinted 1998 (twice).

This is one of **four levels** of Mathematics Assessment Papers for Key Stage 2.

Level 2	ASSESSMENT PAPERS	0 7217 2469 8
	ANSWERS	0 7217 2473 6
Level 3	ASSESSMENT PAPERS	0 7217 2470 1
	ANSWERS	0 7217 2474 4
Level 4	ASSESSMENT PAPERS	0 7217 2471 X
	ANSWERS	0 7217 2475 2
Level 5	ASSESSMENT PAPERS	0 7217 2472 8
	ANSWERS	0 7217 2476 0

Warning

ISBN 0-7217-2476-0

Schofield & Sims Ltd, Huddersfield

9 780721 724768

3

Calculate each of the following.

half of 97	$\frac{3}{4}$ of 76	one third of 84 g	five sixths of 1.74 m
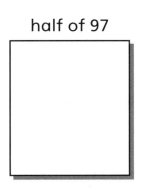	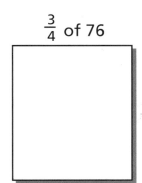	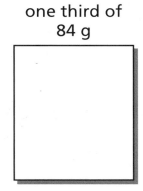	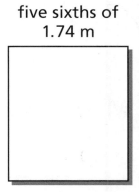

one twelfth of 3 hours	one tenth of 25 litres	five sevenths of 1 week	three tenths of 2 kg
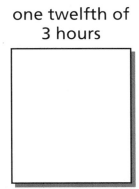	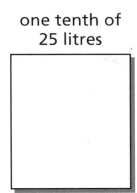		

4

Calculate each of the following.

25% of 300	10% of 35	50% of 18	75% of 12
75	3·5	9	9

20% of 95	$33\frac{1}{3}$ % of 99	$12\frac{1}{2}$ % of 48	5% of 80
19	33	6	4

5

Multiply these numbers by 10.

2.1→ [ ] 2.01→ [ ] 200.1→ [ ] 0.02→ [ ]

Multiply these numbers by 100.

17.0→ [ ] 0.17→ [ ] 1.07→ [ ] 10.07→ [ ]

Multiply these numbers by 1000.

3.04→ [ ] 3.40→ [ ] 0.34→ [ ] 340.0→ [ ]

6

Divide these numbers by 10.

89→ [ ] 809→ [ ] 8.09→ [ ] 8.90→ [ ]

Divide these numbers by 100.

47→ [ ] 4.7→ [ ] 4.07→ [ ] 40.70→ [ ]

Divide these numbers by 1000.

305→ [ ] 3.05→ [ ]

0.35→ [ ] 350.0→ [ ]

A.T.1 – Using and Applying Mathematics   Developing Mathematical language and forms of communication

A.T.2 – Number   Developing an understanding of place value and extending the number system

7

Graph to show maximum and minimum temperatures for one week.

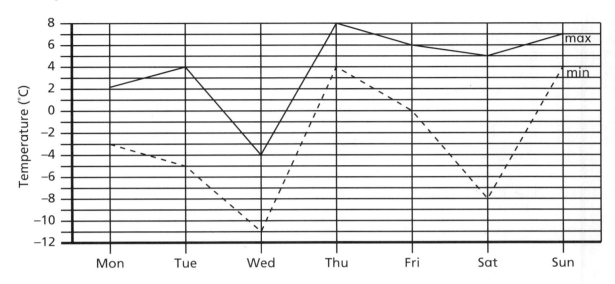

Which day had the biggest temperature range?

What was the mean maximum temperature for the week?

Which day did the temperature not rise above zero?

Complete the following table using the above graph.

Day	Max. Temp (°C)	Min. Temp (°C)	Range	Mean Temp. (°C)
Mon				
Tue				
Wed				
Thur				
Fri				
Sat				
Sun				

8

This square has sides of 1 cm.

Its perimeter is [   ] cm.

This shape is made from 2 of the squares.

Its perimeter is [   ] cm.

The perimeter of this shape is [   ] cm.

Draw the next shape in the series.

Its perimeter is [   ] cm.

Complete the following table.

Number of squares	1	2	3	4	5	6	7	8	9
Perimeter									

What is the perimeter of the shape made with 50 squares?

[   ] cm

How did you work out the answer?

[   ]

If the number of 1 cm squares is **n** and the perimeter of the shape is **P**, write a formula for finding the perimeter of any number of squares in the pattern.

[   ]

9

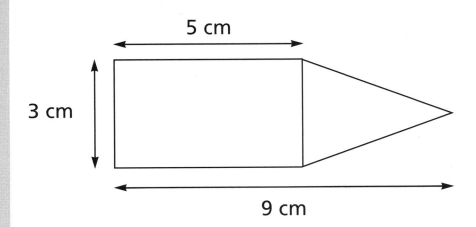

Area of a triangle = $\frac{1}{2}$ (base × height)

Find the area of the triangle shown above.

What is the area of the whole shape?

10

20 g 50 g 2 g   is the same as ⟶ [ ] kilograms

17.3 kg is the same as ⟶ [ ] grams

ml 1000 — 800 — 600 — 400 — 200 —   is the same as ⟶ [ ] litres

27 cm is the same as [ ] metres

[ ] millimetres

10p 2p 5p is the same as [£]

[ ] pence

11

A gardener wishes to make a trellis for his roses.

He needs to buy wooden strips 25 mm wide.

He would like the spaces between the wooden strips to be exactly 20 cm squares.

He would like the finished height to be as near to 2 m as possible.

How high should he make the trellis?
Show your working here.

[ ]

12

Complete the following table and tick whether your estimate is slightly larger or slightly smaller than the Imperial measure.

Imperial measure	rough metric equivalent	The metric measure is slightly larger	slightly smaller
yard			
foot			
inch			
gallon			
pint			
pound			
mile			

An old recipe for a delicious cake gives you all the quantities in Imperial measures. If you wished to make the cake today, what would the rough metric quantities be? Fill in this table.

Imperial	Metric
1 lb flour	
8 oz margarine	
4 oz sugar	
12 oz dried fruit	
$\frac{1}{2}$ pint water	
bake in an 8 inch tin	

13

chocolate biscuits	margarine	apples	milk
6 for £1·08	1 kg for £1·20	loose 56p/lb	1 litre for 58p
8 + 1 free £1·71	500 g for 62p	packs £1·12/kg	1 pint for 29p

Which way of buying each item is the better buy?

Item	better buy	reason
biscuits		
margarine		
apples		
milk		

At the checkout, the bar-code reader is not working properly so the operator enters the items manually.

Your bill comes to £32·40. You only have £10 with you.

What do you do? Explain below.

Your till receipt

```
biscuits          1·08
1 kg apples       1·12
1 pint milk      29·00
1 kg margarine    1·20
total amount     32·40
```

A checkout operator can serve 30 customers an hour.

What is the average time spent per customer?

The average bill per customer is £36·79.
What are the average hourly takings per operator?

At busy times 20 operators are employed.
What are the expected hourly takings at busy times?

One bar-code reader is faulty and the checkout operator can serve only 19 people per hour.
On average, how much is lost by the store per hour?

A.T.1 – Using and Applying Mathematics Making and monitoring decisions to solve problems
A.T.2 – Number Solving numerical problems

11

14

Make a careful drawing of the triangle shown.

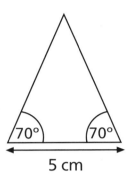

70° 70°

5 cm

How many such triangles would you need
to make a model of a square-based pyramid?

Sketch the net you would use to make the pyramid.
(Ignore any fixing tabs.)

15

Draw all the lines of symmetry on these shapes.

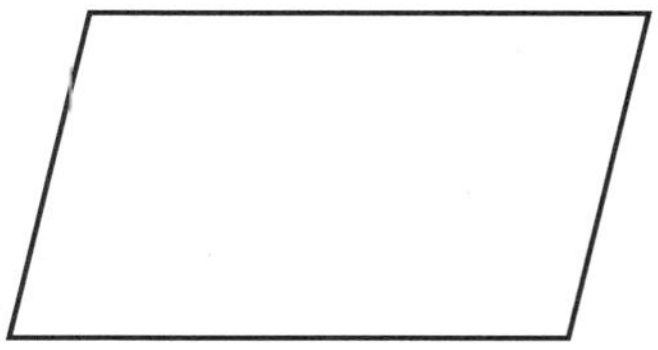

A

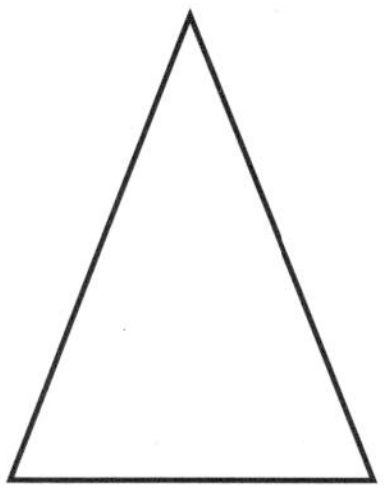

B

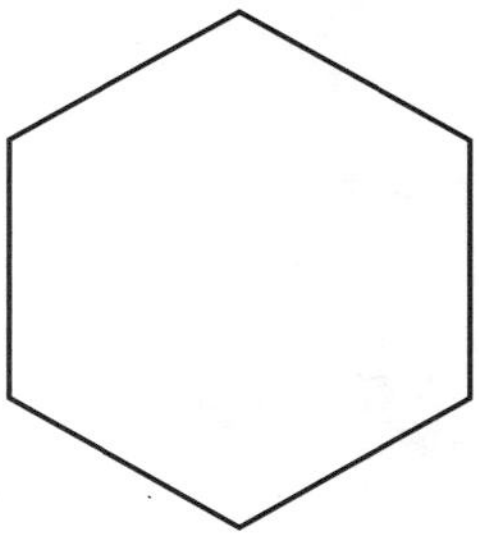

C

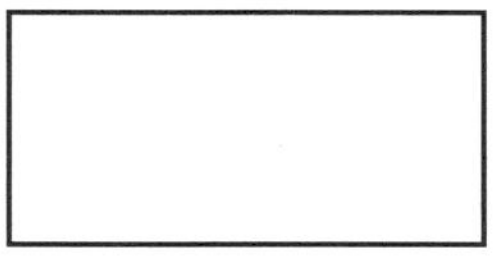

D

E

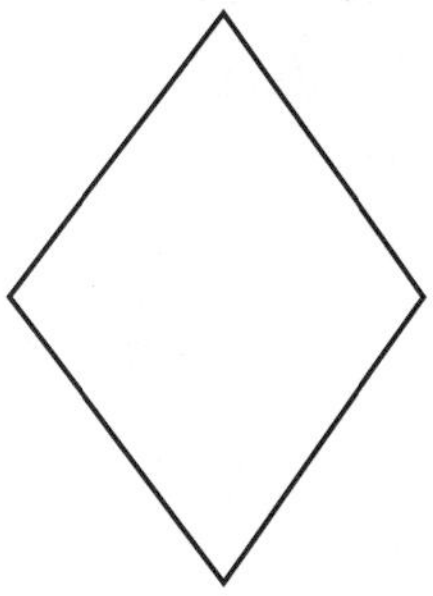

F

Now identify the order of rotational symmetry of each shape and complete the table below.

Shape	Name of shape	Order of rotational symmetry
A		
B		
C		
D		
E		
F		

Which shapes contain obtuse angles?

Which shape contains only acute angles?

16

Class 4 visit the fairground.

Win a teddy
20p a go!

To win a prize,
numbers must
end with '0'

A tombola drum contains all the numbers from 1 to 1000. You can win a teddy if the number you pick ends with zero. If you have a go, what is the probability of winning a teddy?

Show your answer by marking a cross on the scale below.

| 0 | | | | | 0.5 | | | | | 1 |

A stall at the fairground is selling teddy bears.

 Teddy bears
£1·99 each

Amy would really like a teddy more than anything else, but she only has £2·00 to spend.

Should she buy a teddy or hope to win one on the tombola?

Give your reasons.

A.T.4 – Handling Data

Collecting, representing and interpreting data
Understanding and using probability

There are 40 children in Class 4.
This pie chart shows their favourite rides.

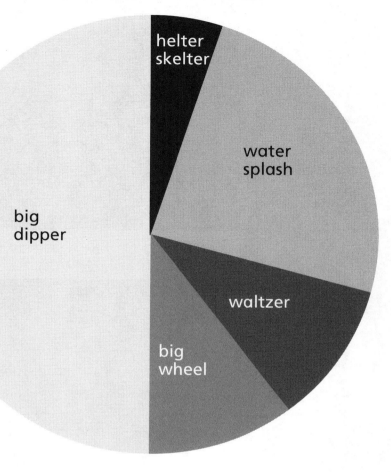

Which ride is the least popular?

What percentage of children
like the big dipper?

Which ride is liked by $\frac{1}{4}$ of
the children?

Which rides are liked by the
same number of children?

10% of the children like
the waltzer.
How many children is this?

These papers are based on the Programmes of Study in **Mathematics** at **Key Stage 2**. They provide a wide variety of assessment opportunities in Mathematics skills, knowledge and understanding.

They are designed as an aid to the teacher's judgement when assessing a child's progress and deciding on levels of achievement. Therefore they should be used within the context of the teacher's knowledge of individual children.

They are not prescriptive in determining levels, but offer valuable indicators to depth and width of ability. Nor are they intended to be sole markers of attainment at any level and it is not anticipated that every child will succeed in every exercise offered in the different skills before being awarded a particular level.

They are a useful aid in planning and in work preparation and differentiation. They also provide a valuable record of progress when informing colleagues or reporting to parents.

Teachers should give help and explanation to children who do not understand initial instructions. Spare paper should be provided for any working out.

First printed 1997.

Reprinted 1998.

This is one of **four levels** of Mathematics Assessment Papers for Key Stage 2.

Level 2

ASSESSMENT PAPERS	0 7217 2469 8
ANSWERS	0 7217 2473 6

Level 3

ASSESSMENT PAPERS	0 7217 2470 1
ANSWERS	0 7217 2474 4

Level 4

ASSESSMENT PAPERS	0 7217 2471 X
ANSWERS	0 7217 2475 2

Level 5

ASSESSMENT PAPERS	0 7217 2472 8
ANSWERS	0 7217 2476 0

Strands covered in Level 5	Page	Date
4 rules to 2 decimal places/check with inverse or approximation	2	
Long multiplication and division (3-digit by 2-digit number)	2	
Calculate fractional parts of quantities/measures	3	
Calculate percentage parts of quantities/measures	3	
Multiply whole numbers and decimals by 10, 100, 1000	4	
Divide whole numbers and decimals by 10, 100, 1000	4	
Compare two distributions, range, mean	5	
Add/subtract negative numbers in context	5	
Construct a formula from a pattern, express a formula in symbols	6	
Use simple formulae (1 or 2 steps)	7	
Convert one metric unit to another	8	
Rough Imperial	9	
Numerical problems as computation	10, 11	
Construct models and draw shapes using angles to the nearest degree	12	
Identify all the symmetries of 2D shapes/ Use angle language	13	
Probability scale 0 to 1/Justify outcomes	14	
Interpret pie charts, draw conclusions	15	

Warning

These publications are *not* part of the copyright licensing scheme run by the Copyright Licensing Agency and may not be photocopied or mechanically copied in any other way, without permission from the publisher.

Schofield & Sims Ltd, Huddersfield

ISBN 0-7217-2472-8